Ellie PAWses

Joan Riedel

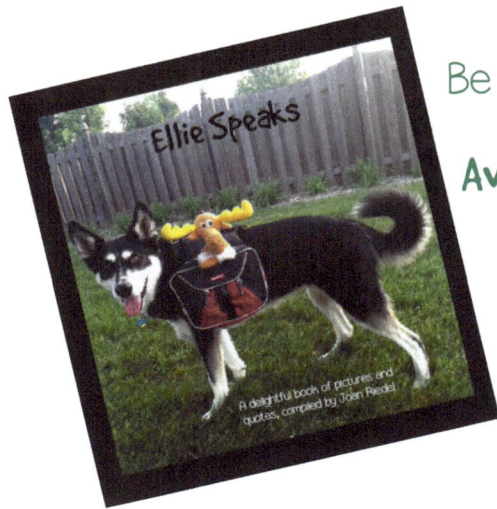

Published by Orange Hat Publishing 2016
ISBN 978-1-943331-13-0

Ellie PAWses

Orange Hat
PUBLISHING

www.orangehatpublishing.com

Dedicated to:

Dad ~ For teaching me by example how to give.

Mom ~ For your unconditional love.

Robert ~ For inspiring me to take more adventures in life.

Mary ~ For always being there for me.

Dick ~ For sharing your music and for our fire talks.

Ron ~ For telling the funniest stories that make me laugh until I cry!

Ellie ~ For choosing us for your family.

"Sometimes you need to give dishes a nap."
~ Jose Andres Puerta

PAWSing . . . Dishes, sometimes I wish I could just let you sleep through the night, but I just can't. 🐾

1

"My favorite thing to make for dinner is . . . reservations!"
~ Unknown

PAWSing . . . That was delicious! May I please see the dessert menu now?

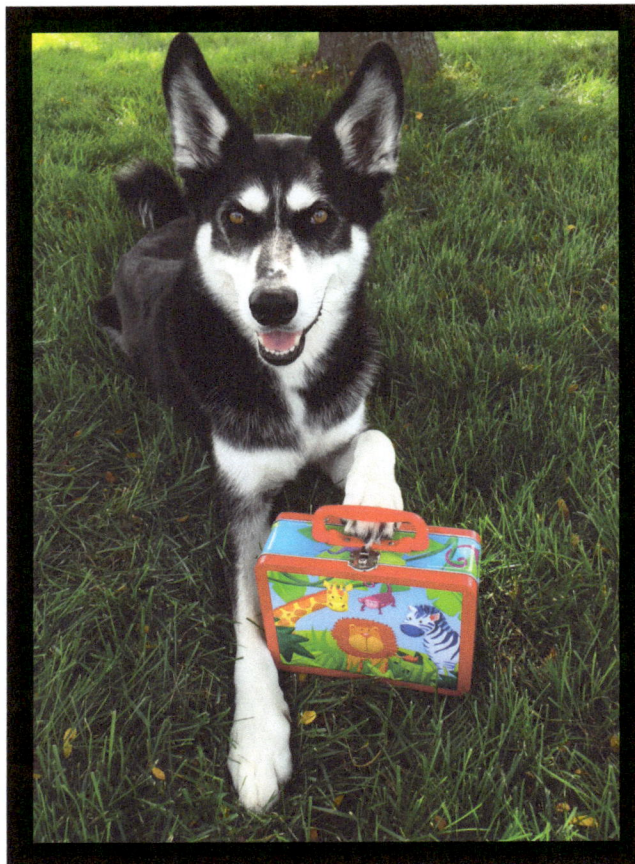

"It is more fun to talk with someone who doesn't use long, difficult words but rather short, easy words like 'What about lunch?'"
~ Winnie-the-Pooh

PAWSing . . . Bone Appetit! 🐾

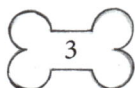

3

"I'm so glad you're here . . . it helps me realize how beautiful my world is."
~ Rainer Maria Rilke

PAWSing . . . forever friendship. Love you, Dom.

4

"Moms. We protect our babies. That's what we do."
~ Unknown

PAWSing . . . Mom! I'm JUST going out to play catch! 🐾

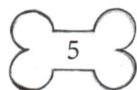

On the green tag in the photo: *llie Riedel Home → Heaven Home Heaven →*

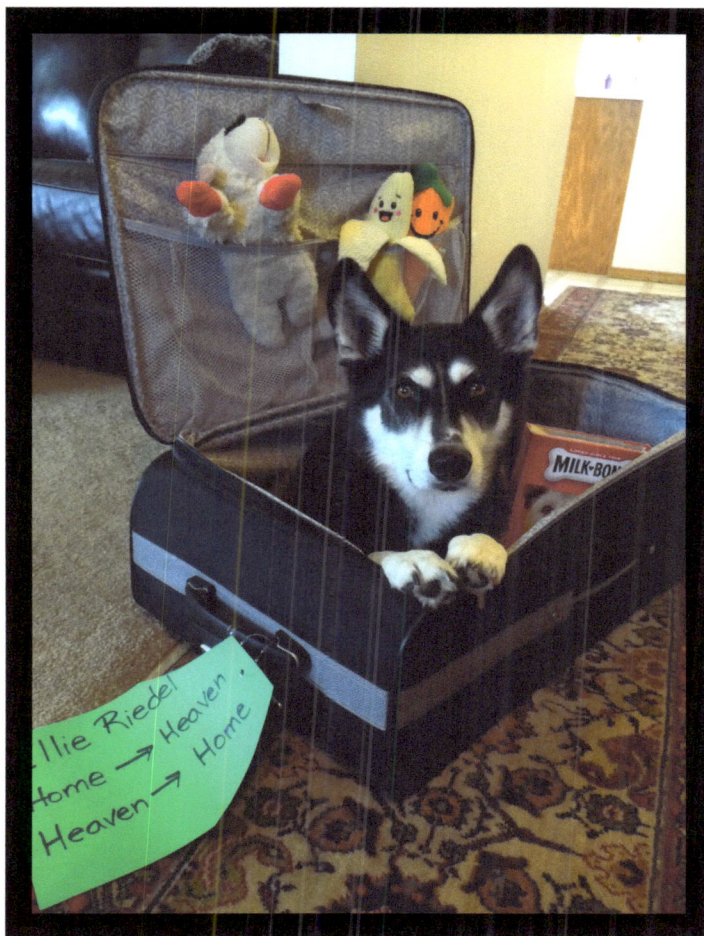

"I wish there were visiting hours in heaven."
                                    ~ Unknown

PAWSing . . . I would love to be able to buy a round-trip ticket to visit the ones I'm missing. 🐾

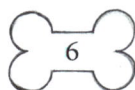

6

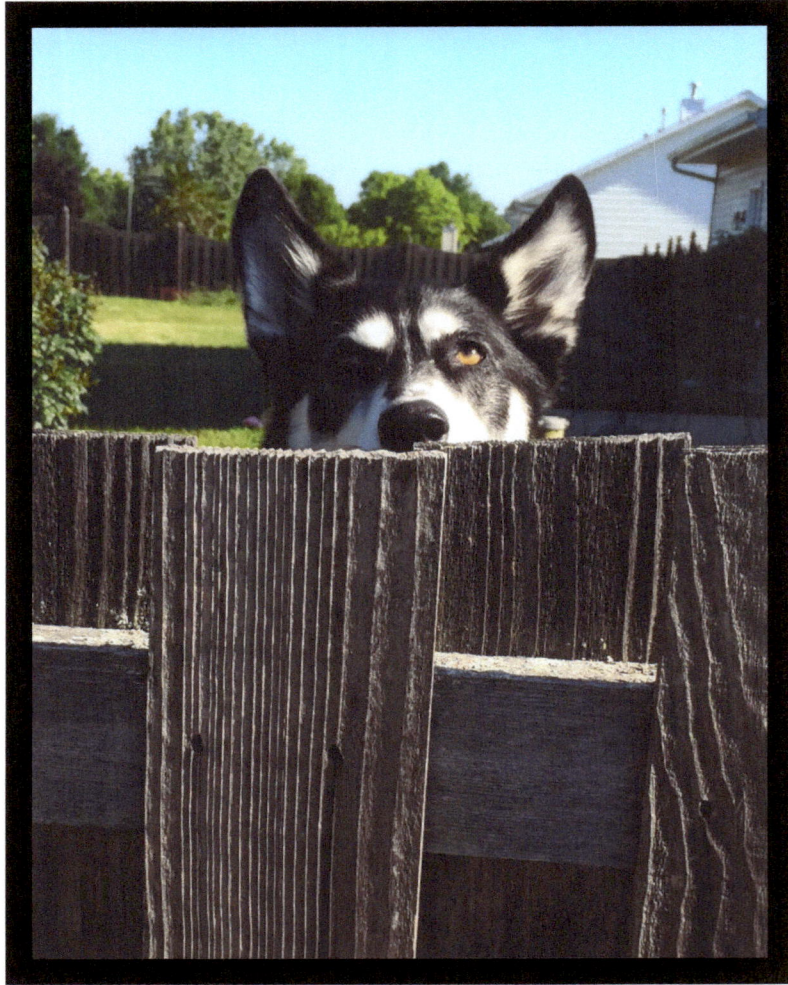

"Wise are those who have seen life from both sides of the fence."
~ A.J. Garces

PAWSing to get a better view of the other side. 🐾

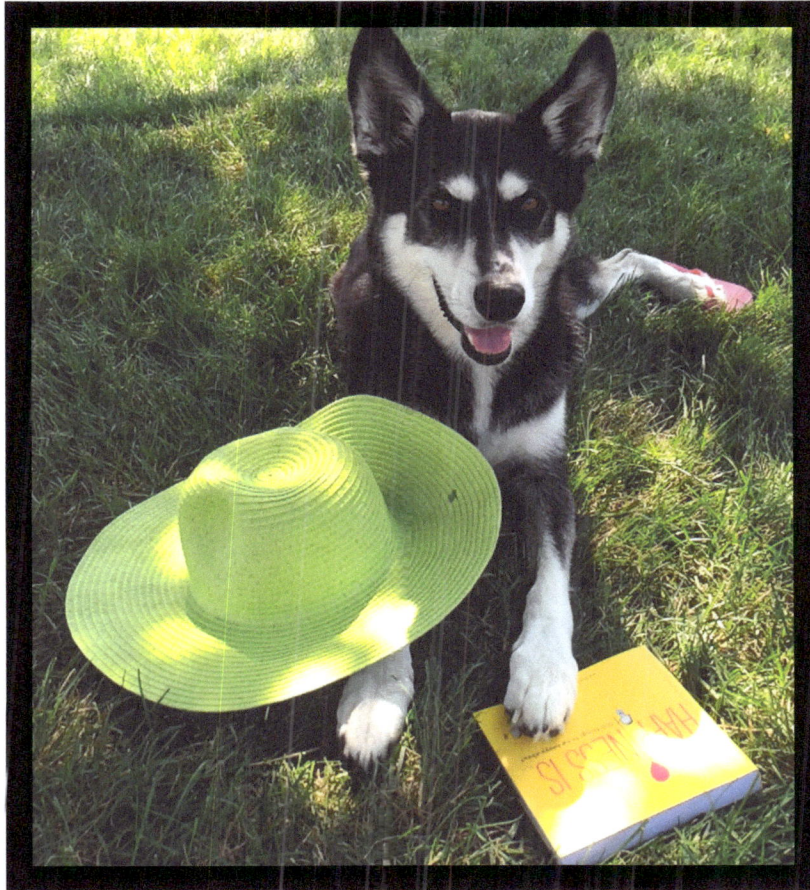

Advice from the Ocean:
Be Shore of Yourself
Come Out of Your Shell
Expand Your Horizon
Don't Get Tide Down
Let Worries Drift Away
Think Big
Live Deep

~ Unknown

PAWSing . . . It's looking like a great day for the beach.

"Never forget to take time for play."
~ Unknown

PAWSing . . . I'm going to hop right to that! 🐾

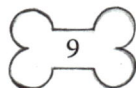

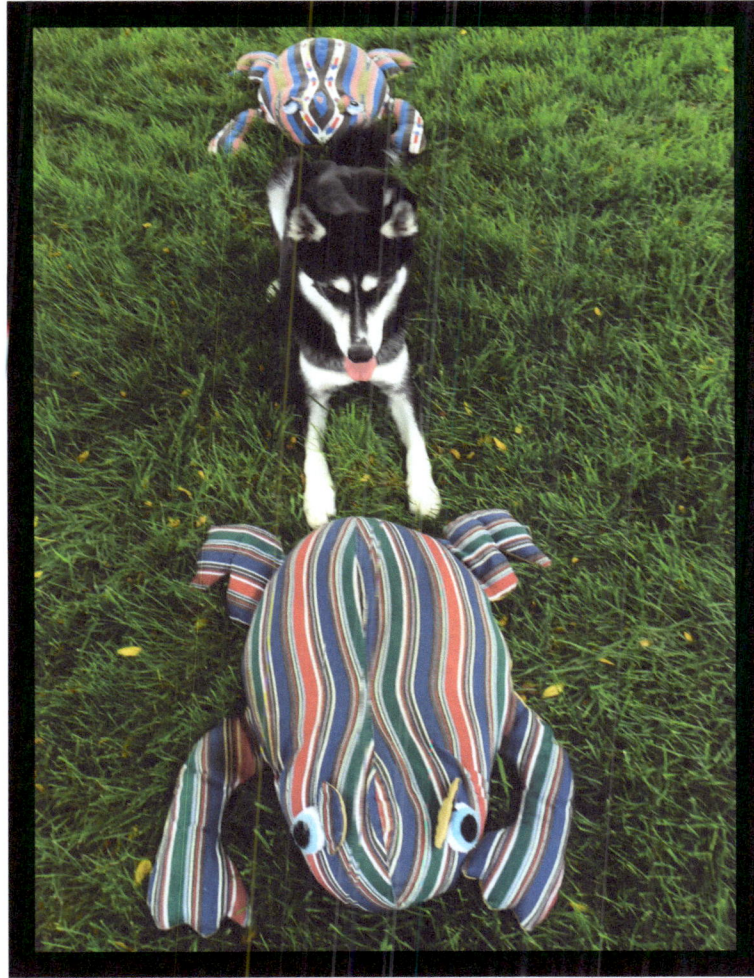

"Play keeps us vital and alive. It gives us an enthusiasm for life that is irreplaceable. Without it, life just doesn't taste good."
~ Lucia Capocchione

PAWSing for a game of leapfrog with Ribbit and Croak.

10

"The most important trip you may take in life is meeting people halfway."

~ Henry Boye

PAWSing . . . Mr. Squirrel, I'm trying to meet you halfway. Please come down and play!

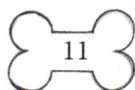

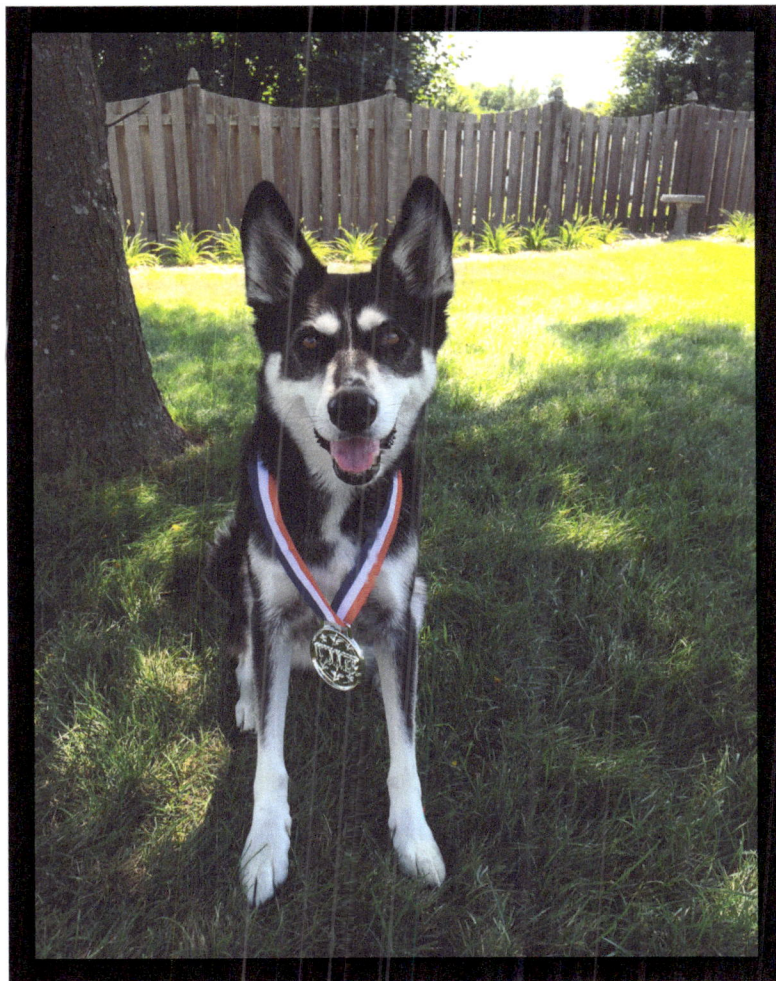

"The extra energy required to make another effort . . . is the secret to winning."

~ Denis Waitley

PAWSing . . . I practically worked my tail off for this. 🐾

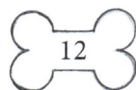

12

"You'd be amazed how often I'm wrong when people say, 'Guess what?'"
~ Unknown

PAWSing . . . okay, I give up. Whooo am I?

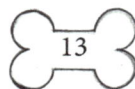

13

"I don't like to do much with my hair – which is good, because I don't know how! I just always make sure I have a great haircut."
~ Chyer Leigh

PAWSing . . . Just a little off the tail today, please. 🐾

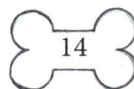

14

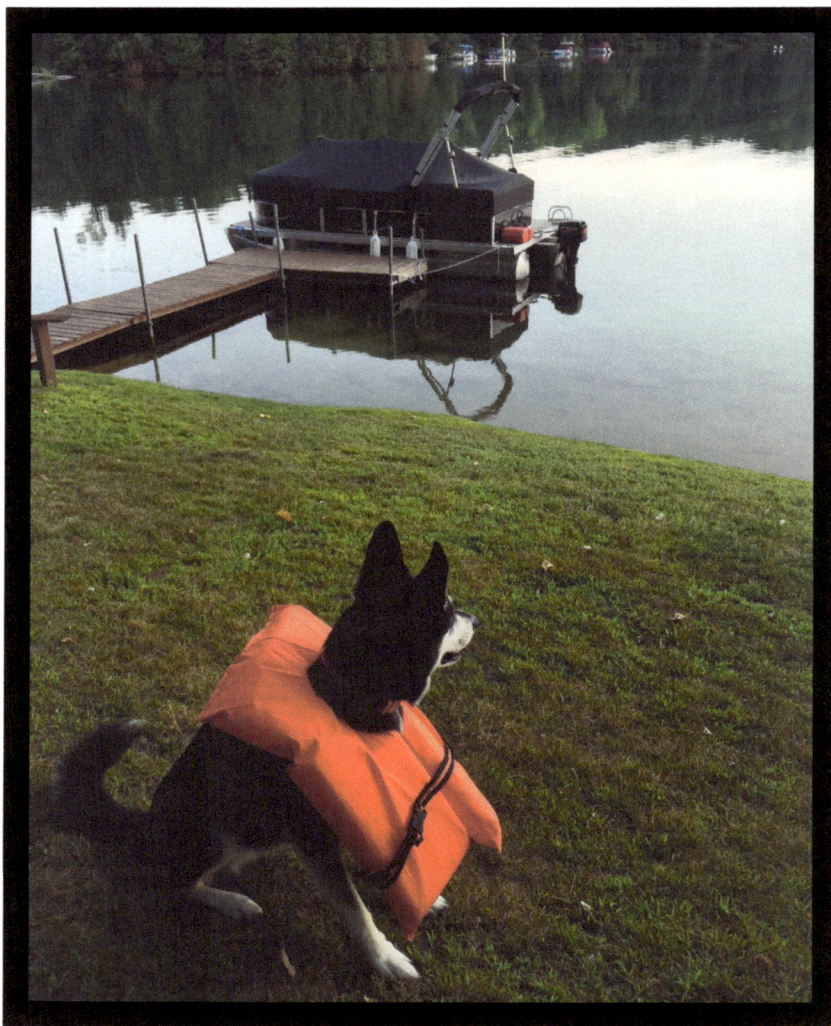

"Life jackets.
They float.
You don't."

~ Unknown

PAWSing . . . Now I just need to find a swimming buddy. 🐾

15

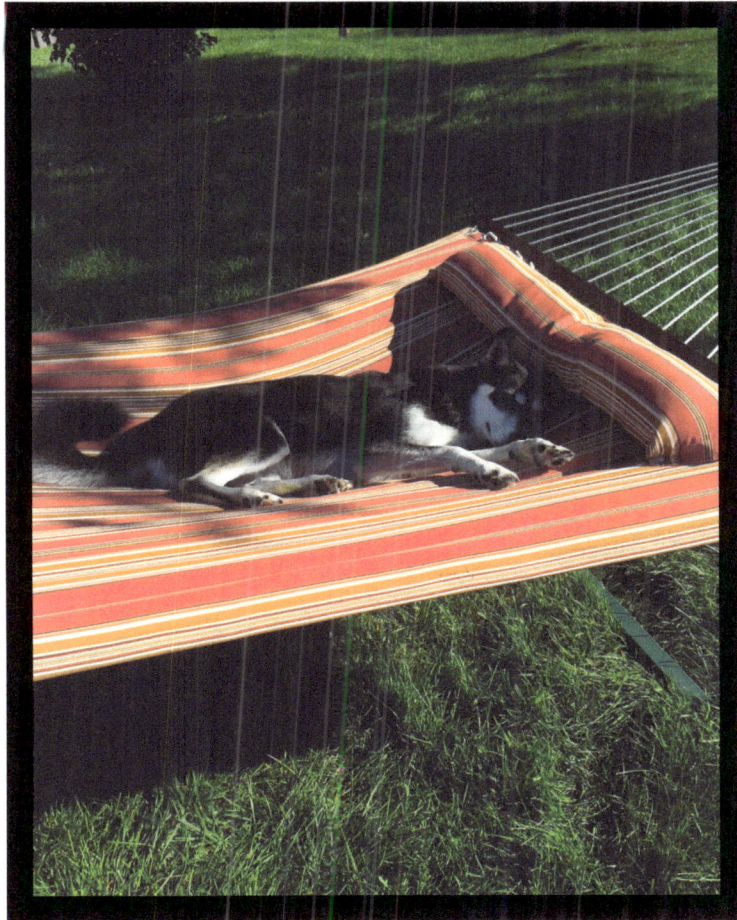

"Your best ideas, those eureka moments that turn the world upside down, seldom come when you're juggling emails, rushing to meet the 5pm deadline or straining to make your voice heard in a high-stress meeting. They come when you're walking the dog, soaking in the bath or swinging in a hammock."

~ Carl Honore

PAWSing . . . Now this is the perfect idea for today!

16

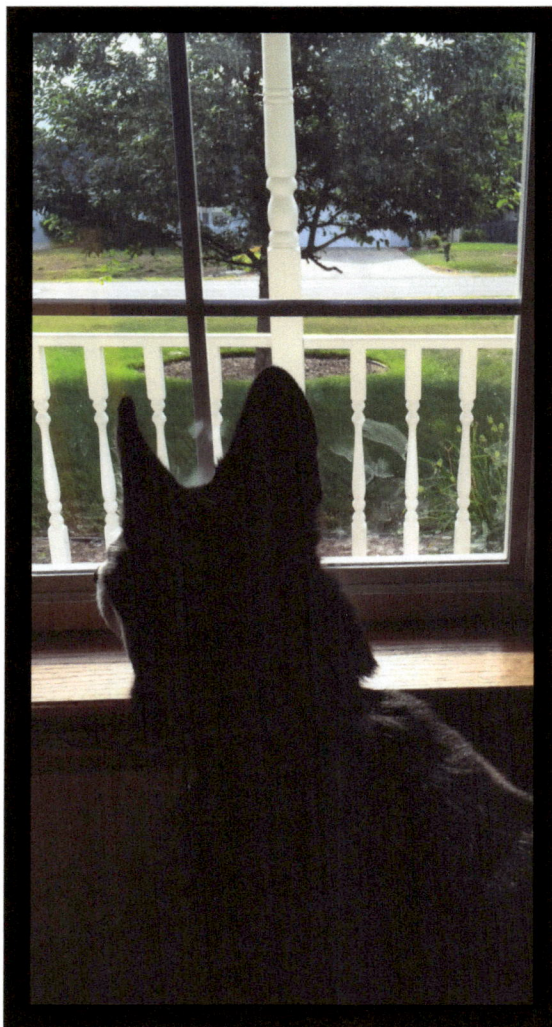

"My windows aren't dirty . . . That's my dog's nose art."
~ Unknown

PAWSing . . . I call this piece "Who Just Walked Past?" My most recent piece, "Birds and Squirrels," can be found in back on the patio door.

"For after all, the best thing one can do
When it *is* raining, is to let it rain."
~ Henry Wadsworth Longfellow

PAWSing . . . Mr. Sun, it is nice to know that you take turns with Mr. Rain.

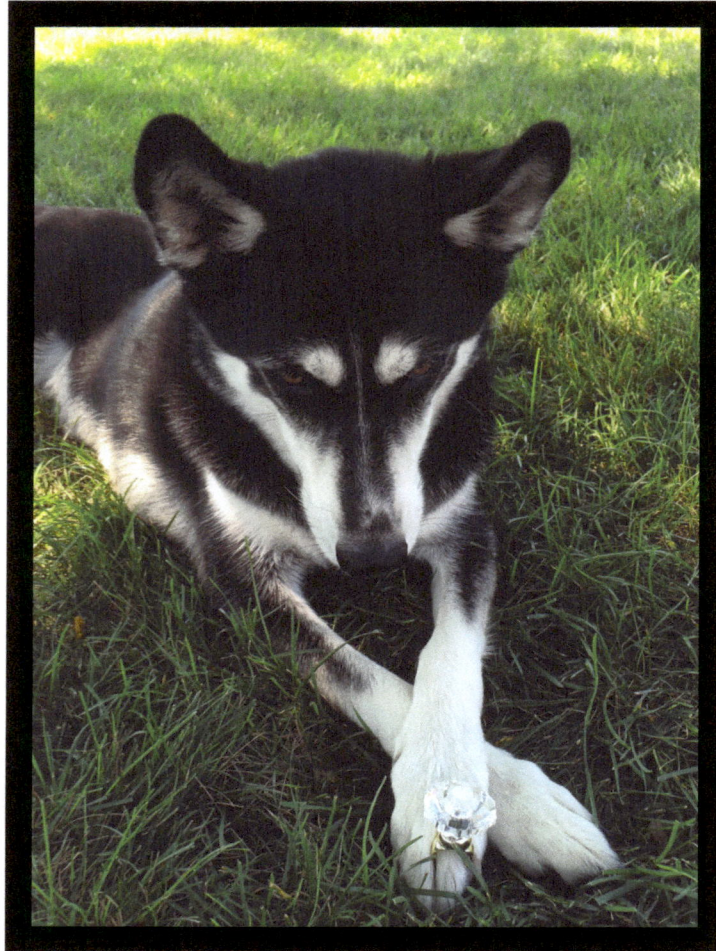

"Love, joy, peace, patience, kindness, goodness, faithfulness, gentleness, and self-control. To these I commit my day."
~ Max Lucado

PAWSing...I do. 🐾

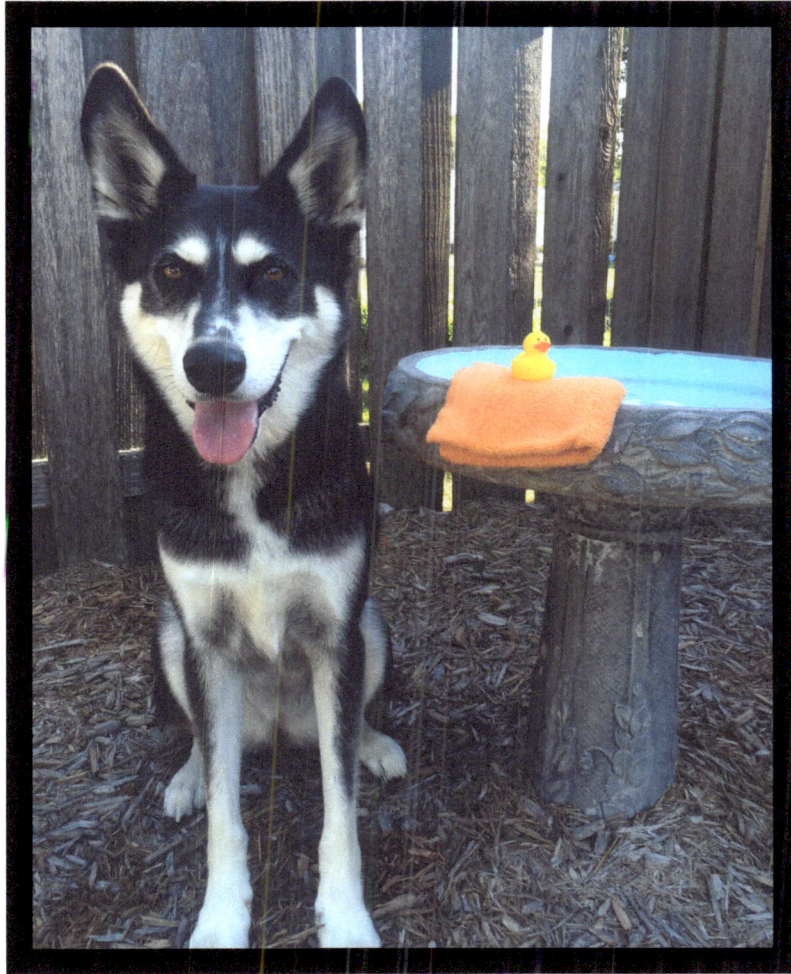

*"The difference between ordinary and extraordinary
is that little extra."*

~ Jimmy Johnson

PAWSing . . . Enjoy your bath today, my feathered friends.

"Cooking is like painting or writing a song. Just as there are only so many notes or colors, there are only so many flavors – it's how you combine them that sets you apart."

~ Wolfgang Puck

PAWSing . . . Mmmmm! Now I just need an added pinch of this and that.

21

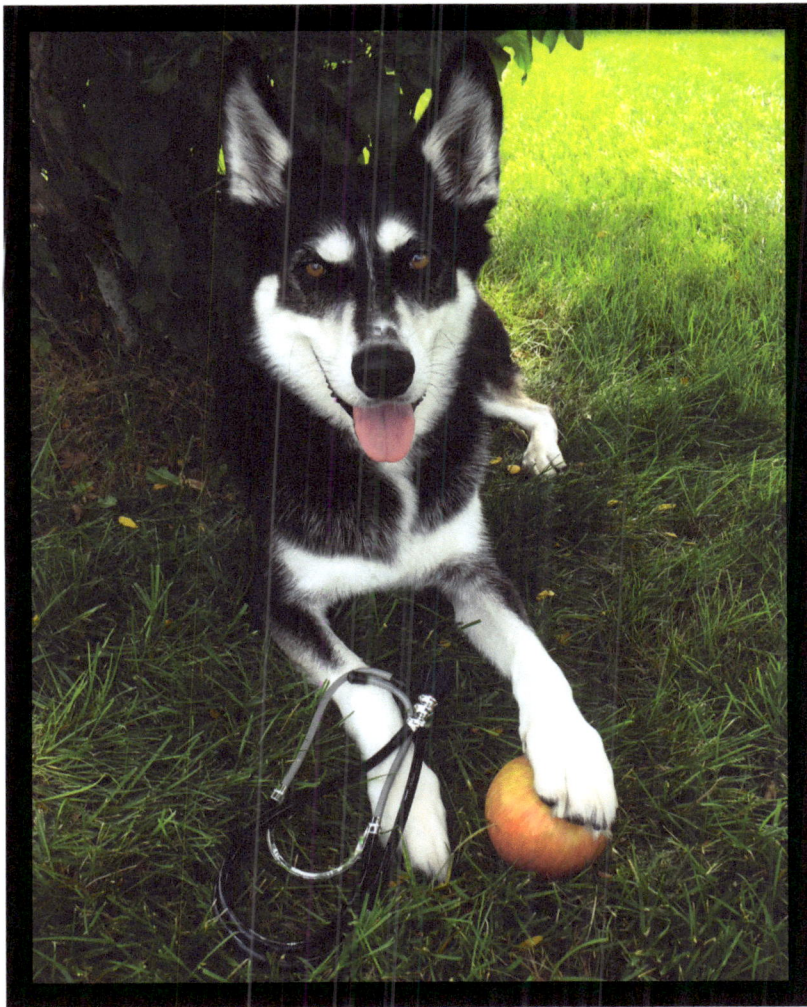

"An apple a day will keep the doctor away.
If the doctor is cute, forget the fruit."
~ Unknown

PAWSing . . . Even if cute, I prescribe daily fruit. 🐾

"Um, no, I haven't seen your crocheting. Have you asked the dog?"
~ Unknown

PAWSing . . . I am absolutely hooked on this!

"Never injure a friend, even in jest."
~ Marcus Tullius Cicero

PAWSing... Hurt a friend? Surely you jest! 🐾

24

"The moment you stop accepting challenges is the moment you stop moving forward."

~ Unknown

PAWSing . . . challenge accepted! 🐾

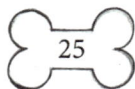

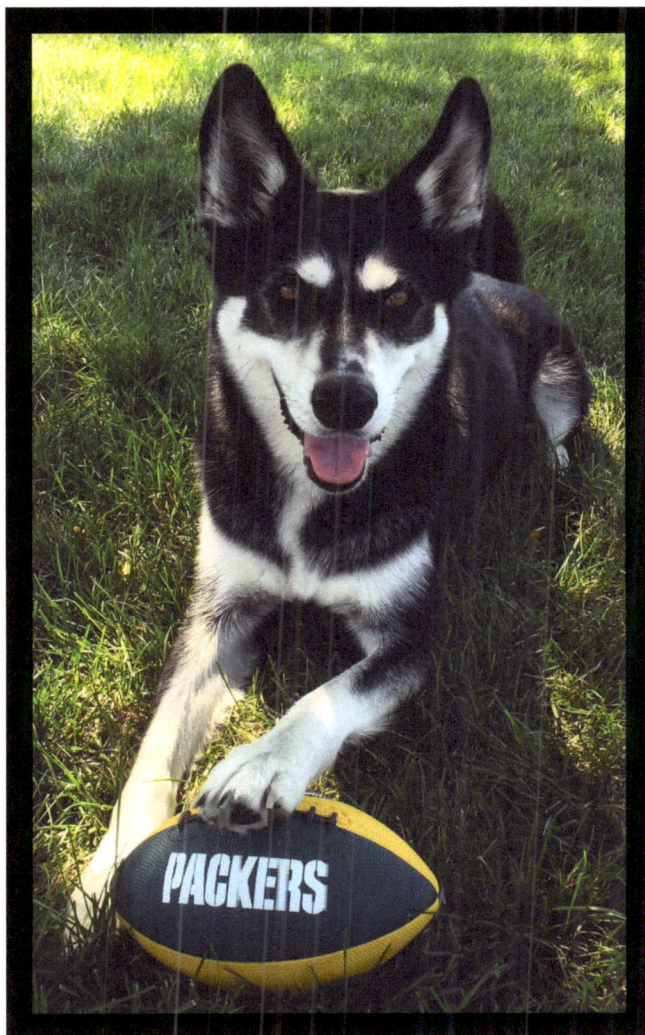

"It's not whether you get knocked down, it's whether you get up."
~ Vince Lombardi

PAWSing . . . I love my Green Bay Packers!

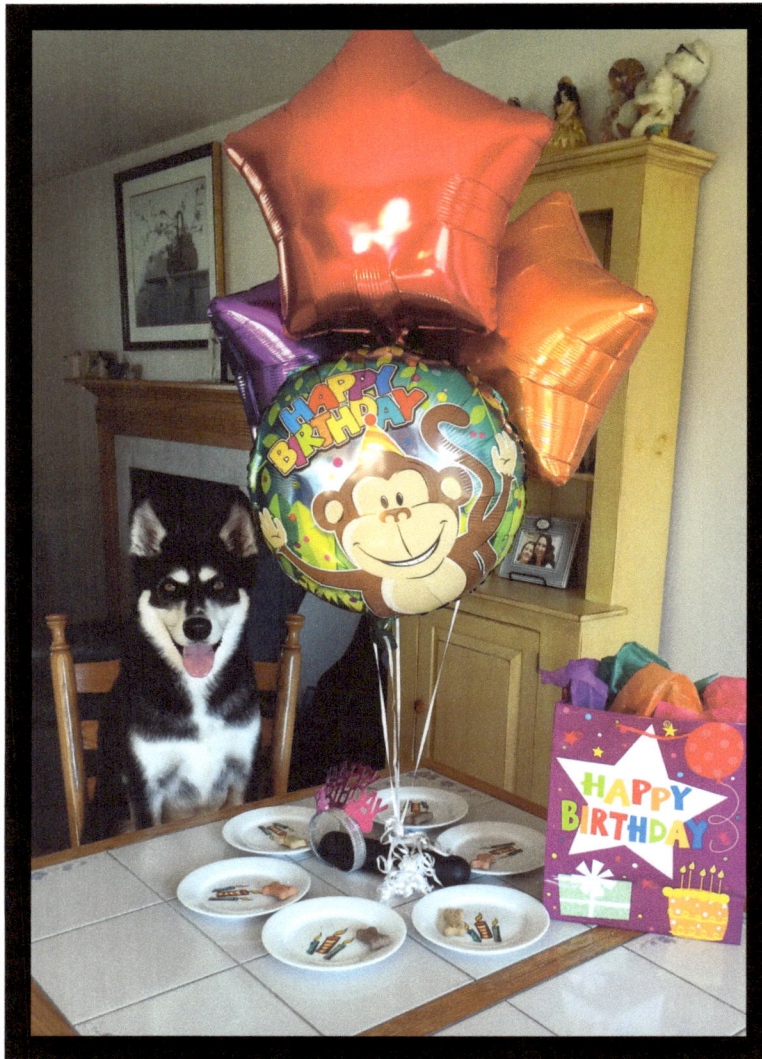

"And in the end, it's not the years in your life that count, it's the life in your years."

~ Abraham Lincoln

PAWSing . . . Today is my birthday and I am living the life!

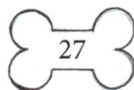

"Reading gives us a place to go when we have to stay where we are."
~ Mason Cooley

PAWSing . . . I am hooked on reading! 🐾

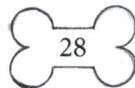

"In golf, as in life, it is the follow-through that makes the difference."
~ Unknown

PAWSing . . . Yay! A perfect hole in one! 🐾

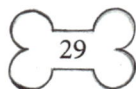

"*Every day is a new day, so live your life with a cherry on top!*"
~ Unknown

PAWSing . . . Pretty, pretty please, may I go to Murphy and Gizmo's house to play today?

"This is a wonderful day. I've never seen this one ever before."
~ Maya Angelou

PAWSing . . . What a sweet day! I hope I see many, many s'more! 🐾

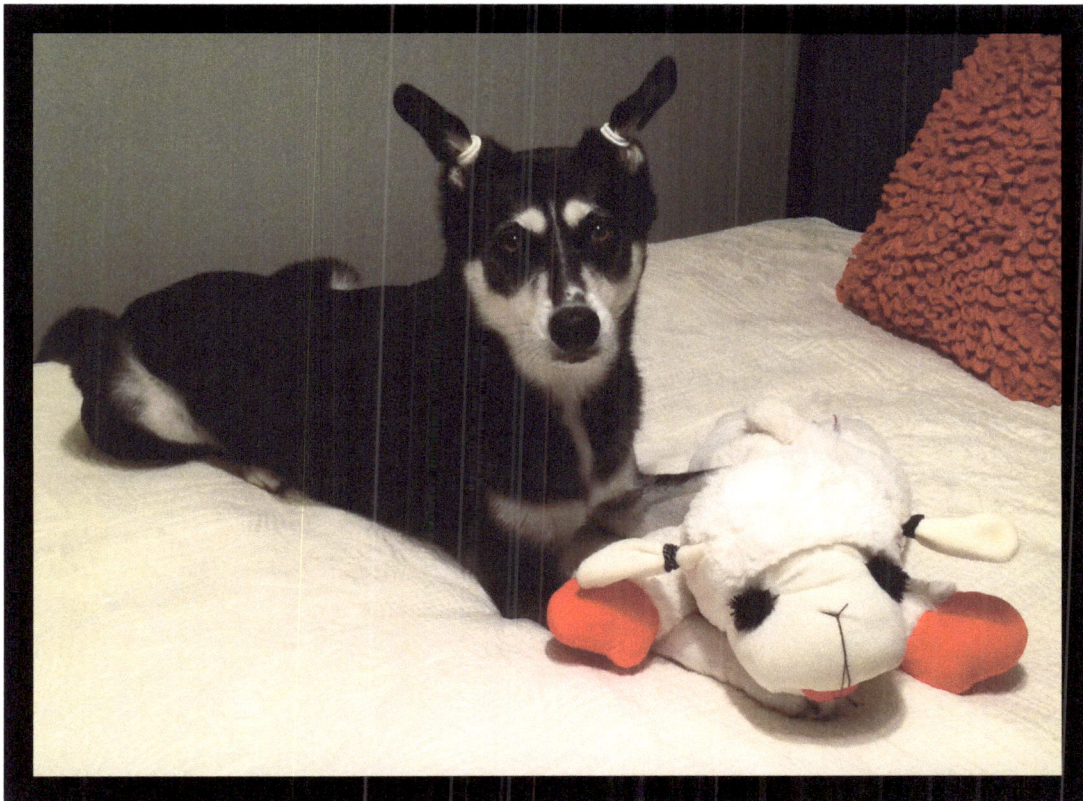

"BEST SLEEPOVER EVER!"

~ Unknown

PAWSing . . . okay, our hair is done. Do you want to do our nails next, Lamby?

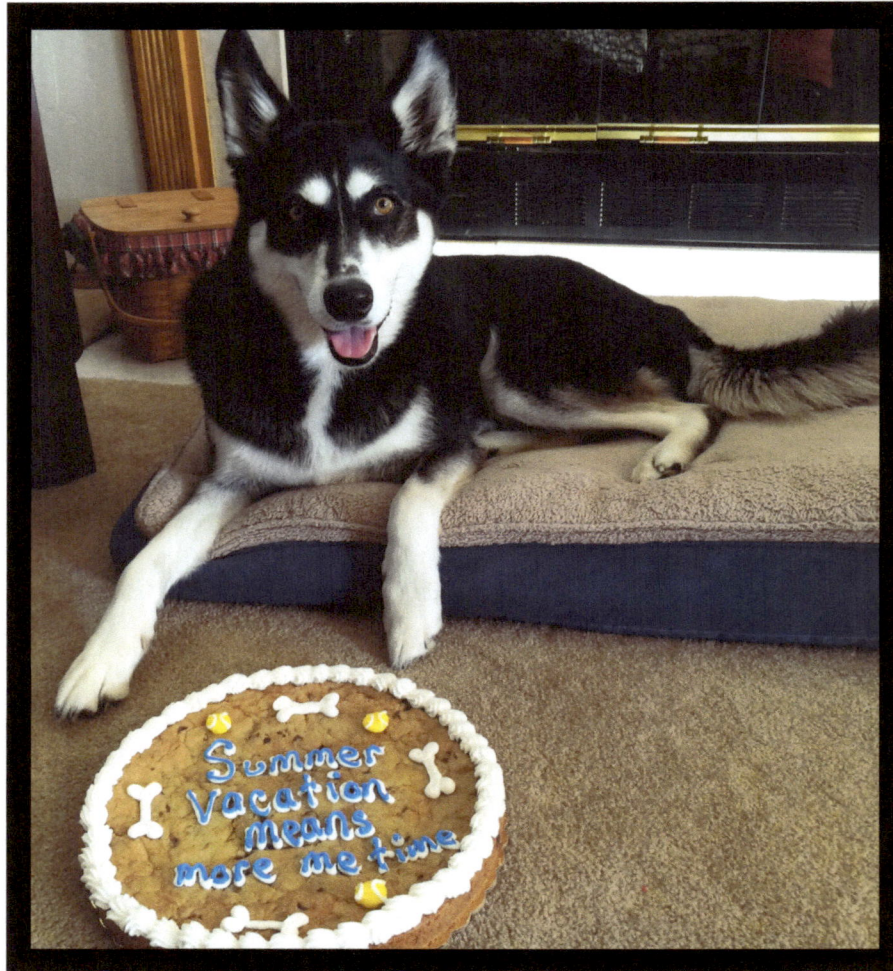

"There is nothing more precious than time."
~ Czech proverb

PAWSing ... Summer with my family is going to be so sweet!

"There is no question that a vinyl record is a lot nicer than a CD . . ."
~ Simon Le Bon

PAWSing . . . So true. I am just here to set the record straight.

"*God is the best listener. You don't have to shout out loud because He hears even the silent prayer of a sincere heart.*"

~ *Unknown*

PAWSing to say my bedtime prayers. 🐾

35

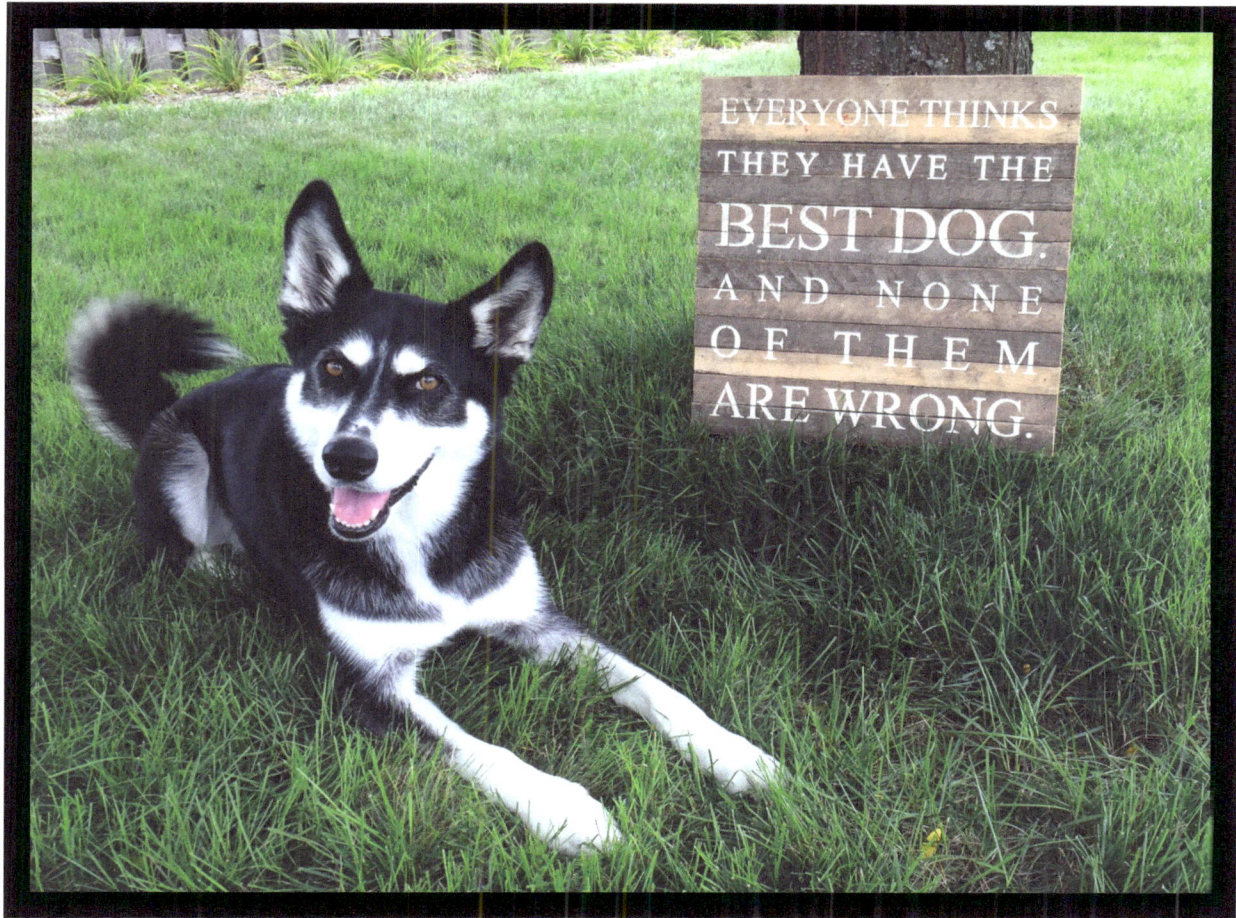

"Nobody can fully understand the meaning of love
unless he's owned a dog."

~ Gene Hill

PAWSing . . . Now that's the truth. 🐾

www.ingramcontent.com/pod-product-compliance
Lightning Source LLC
Chambersburg PA
CBHW041958100426
42813CB00019B/2925